two-by-fours

a sort of serious book
about small children

by **Charles M. Schulz**

and **Kenneth F. Hall**

WARNER PRESS
ANDERSON, INDIANA

Library of Congress Catalog Card No. 65-11355

he is who he is

When a Two-by-Four is a piece of lumber, you can stack it on a neat pile or cut it to just the right length and nail it to a wall. But, the kind of Two-by-Four we discuss here* you can never quite nail down so permanently or stack up so neatly. In fact, these youngsters do not themselves have a clear pic-

---

*Children living in their second, third, and fourth years.

"I've learned to take off my own coat, but it's kind of hard on the buttons!"

ture of just who they are, and they do a lot of groping to try to discover the answer.

No wonder the youngsters have some problems here. One minute we are telling Johnny what a big boy he is and the next we say, "Don't be such a baby!" Someone tells him he looks just like his daddy, and then he gets confused when he looks at that balding patriarch who must be way past twenty years old.

This Two-by-Four has already started on that long process of trying to make himself into a personality different from any-one else, even his parents. To do that he has to bellow "No" to the other person's requests now and then. To emphasize himself he has to do something that will keep him in the lime-light. This may mean getting into mischief, talking loud, and otherwise upsetting adult applecarts. This Two-by-Four just won't stay neatly stacked in a pile.

You see few perpetual frowns on the faces of Two-by-Fours. But, they have a right to be worried, considering all the learn-ing they have to do in a short period of time. These are the years when they have to learn the basic approaches to be taken toward living with other people, learning the tools of simple communication, and polishing the mechanics for sur-vival in such realms as eating and dressing. Fortunately, learn-ing comes easy during this time, the most impressionable years of their lives.

And so the child learns. Just think what it would be like if you were in the small child's shoes again. You wouldn't even know how to lace them. But you would soon have to learn, since most important people know how. Perhaps you wouldn't have

"The way I see it, we die in the same order we were born. . . . It's the only fair way of working it!"

"The first thing I noticed when I walked in here was a first-aid kit. . . . That sort of shook me up!"

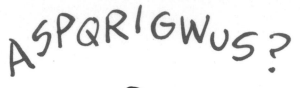

learned yet to like asparagus, but before too many years you would even have to learn how to spell it. And, you would just be starting to learn about sharing.

Fortunately, the child **is** learning and growing. He desperately wants more strength, more status, and more age. This is true even in those moments when he plays like a baby and seeks all the special rights, privileges, and affection pertaining to that status. It reassures a child tremendously to feel that he is growing and will grow some more.

Reassurance plays a considerable role during these years, even as it does for us. Reassurance for the child is finding Mother in the kitchen when he comes toddling out of the bedroom in the morning. It is having the same old beat-up toys lying around him in his room. It is going through the same

8

"The more mature I get, the more childish the rest of the world becomes!"

routine at night——a bath, brushing his teeth, hearing a story, being tucked in bed with a prayer. It is being around adults who themselves are serene, not torn up by the tensions of our insecure world. There is so much that this Two-by-Four does not understand in this big, strange world of ours that he may be frightened deep down inside by something which we would hardly notice.

There are other limitations on the outlook of the small child giving him a view of life different from what we have. You may look a little strange doing it, but try sitting in the middle of the floor in each of your rooms and looking around. It gives you a different perspective, and it moves you in the direction of how a Two-by-Four looks at things. This really gets tricky when it comes to some of the concepts of time and space that we in our ancient wisdom take for granted. Take space, for instance. Out of his background the little child may have a hard time understanding the difference between going ten miles and going a hundred, between living in Ohio and living in Canada. Take time, for instance. How can you understand the difference between a year and a decade when you've never lived a decade or haven't been around long enough to compare one year with the next? How can one person be both a baby and a man?

As he seeks to become a person in his own right, we hope the small child also comes to understand that he is intended to be a child of God. He is fortunate if he lives in the kind of home where God is important——where God is addressed in prayer, where he is read and sung about. As one Two-by-Four said, "I'm glad that God and our family are relations."

"I can never get it through my head. . . . Was Jesus a grown man or was he a little baby?"

"Hi! I've just been told that I'm one of God's children. . . . Who are you?"

it's family life for him

The Two-by-Four is by nature a family man. A night out on the town doesn't appeal to him at all. Travel that takes him away from his family ranks pretty low on his list. The kids around the neighborhood don't begin to compare with his own kin. His family is the center of his universe.

This doesn't mean, of course, that for him h o m e and heaven are the same thing. Most children grow up in families that are somewhat short of divine. Deep down inside himself, the Two-by-Four may be disturbed by things about this home that hardly ever come to the surface. When his daddy or mother are worried about something, he may sense their insecurity even if they don't talk about it in front of him. A hard drive to success and wealth or the frustration that comes with missing such goals may speak with quiet eloquence to him.

At the same time not all these troubles may be so silent. A minor argument between his parents may loom like the opening battle of World War III. Yet, through it all the Two-by-Four usually likes his family, enjoys it in all its imperfections, and somehow manages to grow up into a decent sort of person who looks forward to establishing another family of his own someday.

On the family stage, though, the Two-by-Four likes to be front and center. As a ham actor he is in his glory when the family audience gathers around in rapt attention, with admiration shining in their eyes. He likes to feel that his parents think he's important and has something significant to say. He enjoys feeling that he is a person of influence in this circle.

Unfortunately, there come those moments when he senses that somebody else in the family would like to thrust him out of the spotlight. The threat can come from above, perhaps in the menacing form of Big Brother. This creature not only is taller and stronger but also seems to have special privileges in the family. Maybe this older kid gets to go to school. He gets to stay up later at night, and Dad does more and different things with him. Even worse than all these injustices, however, are the times when the big one hits. He trips up the little one and then with his superior powers of language gets the blame transferred to o u r Two-by-Four. Little wonder,

"Don't try anything on Stanley. . . . He has an overly protective mother who packs a real wallop!"

"I'm proud to say that I am not the least bit jealous of my baby sister. . . . Isn't that perfect proof of a humble spirit?"

then, that the small child develops his own methods of counterattack—running crying to Mother, biting back, or scratching. It is comforting to know that through it all the big and little brothers dearly love each other.

Then there's the threat from beneath. A little n e w kid suddenly appears on the family scene. This baby demands constant care. So cute that even the Two-by-Four likes her himself, she gets rave notices from all the family and the neighbors. But, this arrival suddenly thrusts Two-by-Four out of his beloved spot in the limelight. Let's see, he wonders to himself, what can I do about this? Make friends with the enemy? He tries that. He himself loves this little newcomer, but the response he gets is discouraging. Hit the enemy? Mother would never stand for that. Wage his own publicity campaign? With positive thinking like that, he goes at it. He gets into more scrapes that bring Mother hurrying to check on him. He works all the mischief he can. He tells fantastic stories. What's got into our Two-by-Four? It's really not too hard to understand.

Family life goes on with its daily bumps and bruises. The youngster growing up in a home with wise parents soon discovers that this place is no Society for the Care and Overprotection of Children. He gets plenty of opportunity to spread his wings and try a few test flights. Those crash landings can really hurt, but his parents grit their teeth and endure them. They figure a measure of freedom will help their little one to grow. They know that the empty lot down the back alley can look like Adventureland but that a lot of bravado will disappear when the Two-by-Four is out of sight of the back door. So they're all set for the fluctuating mood between Mama's Boy and Christopher Columbus.

Homes that raise the best Two-by-Fours are centers for discipline. Good old steady, consistent, firm, loving discipline. The Two-by-Four needs to make of discipline a sort of friend whom he would sorely miss if he didn't show up at the right time. Discipline, in a strangely comforting w a y, helps the small child understand the rules of this family game.

If the small child were setting out to pick his own family, he would want one where wise discipline is shown and where he is given a growing sense of responsibility. He'd want a family that would see him as a person in his own right, not just a two-by-four edition of Daddy. He would want a family that knows how to show love wisely and well. He would want a family that points the way to God.

"How could a loving God ever have made big brothers?"

"Whatever happened to the good ol' peaceful Sunday morning breakfast?"

two-by-fours in a wider world

Two-by-Fours are making their first serious ventures out of the safe confines of home into a wider world. Perhaps to them this big world is populated by hurrying young people, loud-voiced men, smothering women, and competitive children. In this bewildering swirl of human relationships, the small child has no backlog of experience to go by. He has had no charm school training. All of a sudden he finds himself out there with those strange people, and he has to start making up his mind what he is going to do about things.

What should be his reaction to these other children? Are they big toys? He pushes, he pulls, he grabs hair. The reaction is not favorable. Some of the adults around seem to expect him to play **with** these children, but that is a procedure that takes some learning. He just can't do it, not right now. He decides that it is fun to play alongside these new friends, but don't ask him to play with them on any sort of give-and-take basis. That is too complex a social situation for him right now.

It is obvious that he needs to learn something about sharing, and this is where he starts taking some early steps toward setting up a satisfactory relationship with other children. He finds that if he lets another child play with his rocking horse for a while, sooner or later he will get it back. In the meantime, some other child may share with him a fire truck

"Just when I was getting strong enough to be able to defend myself, they start telling me about sharing!"

"I think my Grandma would be more understanding if she had a few children of her own."

which, for the moment, seems even better than the rocking horse. He discovers that he who gives in turn receives. There will be ups and downs in the learning process, but learning is under way.

The Two-by-Four is learning all about h o w the pecking order operates among the human species. It is not only in the chicken house that the rooster picks on the largest hen and she turns around and picks on the next one down the line. The big boy with the strong muscles picks on the little one.

"We have a Sunday school teacher who talks pretty loud."

The character with lots of fight and fizz picks on the quiet, shy one. It's just too bad to be at the low end of the pecking order. Yet, this is precisely where many Two-by-Fours are when they start out into the big wide world. And this may be where they try to put the other fellow when they get the chance.

The approach of some strange adults can put fear into the heart of the most courageous Two-by-Four. Some over-powering adults move in on a child at high speed on what looks like a collision course. But this does not quite happen. At the last minute the head-on approach blossoms into a great, smothering hug or a hearty jab in the ribs accompanied by booming voice. These people mean to be friendly, but they leave the Two-by-Four overwhelmed. They leave him trying to protect himself from these intrusions. Most small children would prefer a rather quiet, kindly, gentle approach. That leaves them free to make the noise and do the jabbing.

This wider world is at heart an adult world all hemmed in by adult notions of behavior. It imposes a near-angelic standard on youngsters, who at last report had not yet been issued their halos. Most adults know that it is impossible for a healthy Two-by-Four to sit still. They know he has big muscles to exercise, a voice to call with, a galloping mind to keep occupied, and only limited conviction that the expectations of adulthood are meant for him. But some adults forget. And Two-by-Fours sometimes fail on their best intentions.

The magic word that smooths out the rough moments and forms a solid basis for the small child's relationships with other people is not "alakazam". The word is "love." The Two-

26

"God loves me. . . . God loves me not. . . . God loves me. . . . God loves me not. . . ."

by-Four needs to be reminded constantly that he is loved. If he feels that another person loves him, he will readily accept that person into his own life. Happy is the child who feels that his parents love him, that the young people he meets love him, that the neighbors love him, that all the people down at the church love him. Happy is that child, for in this way he also can begin to know something of God's love for him.

"Where are all the hypocrites? I've always heard that the church is filled with hypocrites."

"My name is Walter. . . . I'm three years old, and I've come to get religion!"

when two-by-fours go to church

If you were a small child and were to look around some church buildings, you might almost get the notion that you weren't welcome. The pews don't fit. The sermon doesn't fit. The songs don't fit. Only over in a dusty corner under the basement stairs has some kind of nursery been set up for you. Everywhere the grown-ups look stiff and somber, and they frown at you when you drop your dime for the offering.

Fortunately, this isn't a true picture of most churches these days. Oh, the pews in the sanctuary may still not fit, and the sermon may not fit. After all, the church does have to minister to some full-sized people, too. But the church that takes seriously its ministry to all people does try to serve the youngest people who come to it.

The church sets out to say to Two-by-Fours, "Our church is such a happy place." The place where nursery children come on Sunday morning is just as bright and beautiful as people in the congregation can make it. Nursery workers, dressed in their neatest, most cheerful clothes, try to make the small child welcome, help him feel that he really matters, and that this is a place where it is fun to be. There are men here because we don't want the small child to grow up feeling that church is just a place for women and children. Both men and women work here, too, because this service is just as important as can be offered anywhere else.

A real sense of purpose governs the situation as t h e s e nursery children come together on Sunday morning. This is

"One more songbook, and I think I'll almost be able to see the preacher. . . ."

"There it is! That's MY church! Well, I don't exactly mean it's MY church. . . . What I mean is that it's MY church. . . . Well, you know what I mean."

not just a glorified baby-sitting service. Here they find adults who really love them and accept them, no matter how they act. The activities are satisfying to the children, not just busy-work to keep idle hands and voices from upsetting the rest of the studying, worshiping congregation. The adults serving here know how to use pictures and stories, music and play-time activities to keep things from getting dull. If a dozen jets fly overhead, these leaders are ready to change their plans to tie in with the children's interests of the moment.

What can you teach a child as small as a Two-by-Four? Don't expect too much——for right now; don't accept too little ——for the future. And don't expect these moments at the church to do what really should be done in the home, which is still the focal point of the small child's life. Yet, the small child is learning at church that people do talk with God, that the Bible is an important book, and that Jesus loves boys and girls. Church begins to seem important. Down under-neath are boiling those great, profound questions he may soon be asking outloud: Where did I come from? Why was I born? Will God punish me if I am bad? Why did our neighbor die? The basis for sound answers to questions like these is being laid here.

The child learns in a way he may never leave behind that God loves him. He may sometimes be lonely, but God still cares. When the cat scratches, God loves him. Alone at night, he remembers that God loves him. It may only have been a simple song he used to sing at church when he was barely able to walk on his two feet, but it has been an experience to go with him through the years.

34

"I was under the impression that when you looked out of this church window, you'd be able to see Jerusalem. . . ."

The church building is an interesting place to the small child, quite different from his home. He loves to explore the place. He learns that there is no danger of the minister pushing the pulpit over, after all. He discovers what the organ pipes sound like up close. He finds out that the minister has an office lined with books where he prepares his sermons and talks with people who need help. He learns all about the supplies the janitor u s e s to keep the place clean and shining. He comes to love the building as a sort of second home, and he recognizes that in some special way it is God's house, too.

The Two-by-Four may not understand everything he hears at church. But across the weeks and months he learns to love it. He knows that it is an important place where grown-ups come to be with each other to worship God, and to learn how better to serve God's cause.

Small wonder that so many Two-by-Fours these days begin asking their mothers on Monday morning, "Is tomorrow church day?"

"Don't cry so loud. . . . We're trying to sing, 'Our Church Is Such a Happy Place.'"

"They're starting to pray again. . . . This is where we came in."

"We were singing, 'Jesus Loves Me' when all of a sudden it hit me. . . . Jesus loves me . . . ME . . . completely worthless ol' me!"

"I think I'm beginning to understand. . . . Going to church is something like having a night-light!"